Mud, Grass, and Ice Homes

Debbie Gallagher

Smart Apple Media

Smart Apple Media
2140 Howard Drive West
North Mankato, Minnesota 56003

First published in 2007 by
MACMILLAN EDUCATION AUSTRALIA PTY LTD
627 Chapel Street, South Yarra, Australia 3141

Visit our Web site at www.macmillan.com.au or go directly to www.macmillanlibrary.com.au

Associated companies and representatives throughout the world.

Copyright © Debbie Gallagher 2007

Library of Congress Cataloging-in-Publication Data

Gallagher, Debbie, 1969-
    Mud, grass, and ice homes / by Debbie Gallagher.
    p. cm. — (Homes around the world)
    Includes index.
    ISBN 978-1-59920-154-2
    1. Dwellings—Juvenile literature. 2. Earth construction—Juvenile literature. 3. Grass huts—Juvenile   literature. I. Title.

TH1421.G35 2007
728—dc22

                                        2007004646

Edited by Angelique Campbell-Muir
Text and cover design by Christine Deering
Page layout by Domenic Lauricella
Photo research by Legend Images
Illustration by Domenic Lauricella

Acknowledgements
The author and the publisher are grateful to the following for permission to reproduce copyright material:

Cover photograph: Pueblo home © iStockphoto.com/John Sfondilias.

© Craig Lovell/Eagle Visions Photography/Alamy, p. 18; © Kirsty McLaren/Alamy, p. 26; © Breck/Dreamstime.com, p. 30 (center left); © Brownm39/Dreamstime.com, p. 30 (bottom right); © The DW Stock Picture Library, Sydney, p. 4; © Getty Images/Stone/Stuart Westmorland, p. 11; © Peter Hickson, p. 25; © iStockphoto.com, p. 5; © iStockphoto.com/Eric Bechtold, p. 30 (top right); © iStockphoto.com/Marje Cannon, p. 24; © iStockphoto.com/Jacques Croizer, p. 30 (top left); © iStockphoto.com/John Sfondilias, pp. 1, 6 (center), 13; © Lonely Planet Images/Richard I'Anson, p. 16; © Lonely Planet Images/Robyn Jones, pp. 6 (bottom), 19; © Lonely Planet Images/Ariadne Van Zandbergen, p. 12; © Dana Smillie/Saudi Aramco World/ PADIA, p. 22; © Mark Moxon, www.moxon.net, p. 30 (bottom left); © Michael Spencer/Saudi Aramco World/PADIA, pp. 3, 7 (top), 20, 21, 23, 30 (center right); © Photodisc, pp. 7 (bottom), 27; © Photolibrary.com, p. 15; © Photolibrary/Index Stock Imagery, p. 14; © Photolibrary/Oxford Scientific Films, p. 17; © Photolibrary/Peter Arnold Images Inc., p. 9; © Photolibrary/ Photo Researchers, Inc., pp. 6 (top), 8, 10.

While every care has been taken to trace and acknowledge copyright, the publisher tenders their apologies for any accidental infringement where copyright has proved untraceable. Where the attempt has been unsuccessful, the publisher welcomes information that would redress the situation.

Contents

Glossary words

When a word is printed in **bold**, you can look up its meaning in the glossary on page 31.

Shelter

Everyone needs shelter, as well as food and water, warmth, and protection. Homes around the world provide shelter for people.

This is a grass home in Papua New Guinea.

People live in many different types of homes.
Some homes are made of mud, grass, or ice.

These homes have mud walls and grass roofs.

Mud, grass, and ice homes

Homes made of mud, grass, or ice are built with materials found in the local area.

Inuit people build igloos made of snow and ice.

Adobe homes made from mud are found in many countries.

People around the world live in homes made from grass and straw.

Mud and grass homes often take a long time to build. Sometimes they are decorated with special designs.

In southern Iraq, the Ma'dan people live in reed houses built on mud islands.

Mud bricks are used to build houses in cities and in the country.

Igloo

An igloo is a home made of snow and ice. Inuit people in the **Arctic** build igloos during hunting and fishing trips.

Sometimes several igloos are built close together.

Blocks of snow are placed in a circle. Each block is a bit bigger than the one underneath and leans inward. This **spirals** around to make a **dome**.

entrance

long knife for cutting blocks

rectangular blocks leaning inward

Igloos are quick and easy to build.

Inside an igloo

Inside an igloo there are shelves of snow. These are covered with furs for sitting or sleeping on. Two igloos can be joined by a tunnel to add another room.

furs on snow shelf

smooth inside walls

ice-block window

lamp

Lamps are used inside the igloo for light.

The doorway faces away from the wind. This keeps the cold air from blowing into the igloo. The inside melts a little and then refreezes, making the igloo stronger.

The igloo's doorway arches downward to keep heat from escaping.

Adobe home

More than a billion people around the world live in adobe homes. In southwestern United States they are called pueblo homes.

In Africa, the Dogon people live in adobe villages.

Adobe homes are made from sun-dried mud bricks. The walls are covered with wet mud. Sometimes the outside walls are decorated with paint or carvings.

small windows

flat roof

ladder access to roof

door

outdoor adobe oven

The flat roof is made using logs and mud.

Inside an adobe home

Inside an adobe home there are rooms for storage, working, and living. In places where it is very hot, the family may sleep outside on the roof.

adobe wall

wood used for fuel

long-handled tools

outdoor oven with fire

Cooking is sometimes done in an outside oven.

Window and door openings are small and walls are thick. This keeps the inside temperature more comfortable than outside.

An open fire is used for heating when it is cold.

Grass hut

Many people around the world live in **traditional** grass huts. Some are made entirely of grass and branches or reeds. Others have grass roofs with mud-brick walls.

Grass huts can be grouped together to make villages.

Grass huts are made by attaching grass or straw to a frame of wood or reeds. The grass might be woven together to make **thatch**, or knotted onto the frame.

grass covering

beehive shape

house frame

The frame is made from wood or reeds.

Inside a grass hut

There is usually only one room inside a grass hut.
In larger huts screens separate different areas.
Cooking and other jobs are often done outside.

screened wall

beams to support the roof

grass thatch roof

woven grass walls

The beams inside this home are decorated with traditional artwork.

Grass huts are strong. Powerful winds can blow right through them without causing any damage.

The grass covering can be knotted or woven into beautiful designs.

Ma'dan reed home

In southern Iraq, Ma'dan families live in homes made from reeds. Reeds are tall, straight grasses that grow in **marshes**. The homes are built on islands of mud.

The Ma'dan people use boats to travel around the islands to different homes.

Long reeds are tied together to make poles. These are bent to make an arch. Mats made from woven reeds are laid over the frame.

reed pole arches

reed bundles

It takes several days to build a Ma'dan reed house.

Inside a Ma'dan reed home

Inside a Ma'dan reed home there is one large room. The floor is made of reed mats. A space in the middle is left bare for the cooking **hearth**.

tied reed poles

woven mat wall coverings

rugs

The floor is covered with rugs.

Reed houses do not last long in the marshes. Luckily, reeds grow quickly so the Ma'dan build new homes whenever they need to.

Ma'dan reed homes are beautifully decorated.

Modern mud-brick house

Some families in cities and in the country live in modern mud-brick houses. These homes use new materials and new ways of building. They do not look like traditional adobe homes.

This modern mud-brick home has a layer of mud smoothed over the bricks.

Mud bricks are made in a big **mold**. Mud is poured into the mold and flattened by a bulldozer. Some **asphalt** is mixed into the mud to make the bricks stronger.

windows

mud-brick walls

These traditional mud bricks are made from mud, clay, and straw.

Inside a modern mud-brick house

Inside a modern mud-brick house there may be many rooms. Sometimes there is a central fireplace for heating. The concrete floors are covered with carpet, stone, tiles, or lumber.

wooden frame

lumber lining inside walls

central brick fireplace

stone floors

Inside walls can be painted or plastered.

Mud-brick houses use mostly local materials. Other materials, such as glass and lumber, are sometimes used as well.

These mud-brick walls look similar to the natural area behind the home.

Floor plan

This is the **floor plan** of an adobe home. It gives you a "bird's-eye view" of the rooms inside the home.

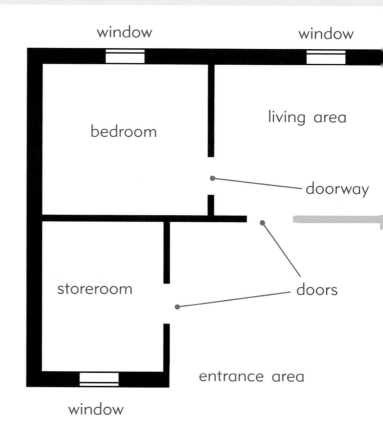

window

window

living area

bedroom

doorway

doors

storeroom

entrance area

window

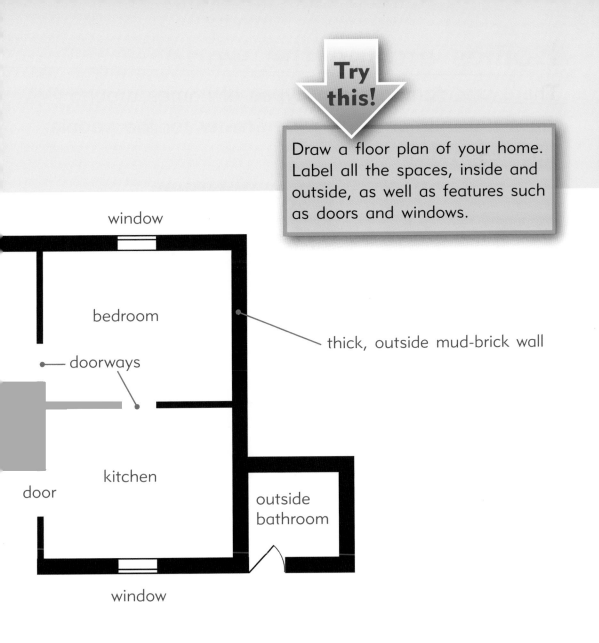

window

bedroom

doorways

thick, outside mud-brick wall

door

kitchen

outside
bathroom

window

Draw a floor plan of your home.
Label all the spaces, inside and
outside, as well as features such
as doors and windows.

Homes around the world

There are many different types of homes around the world. All homes provide shelter for the people who live in them.

A pit home in Africa

New York City apartments

Windsor Castle in London

Mud and grass homes

Tuareg tent in the
Sahara Desert

Lake home in Asia

Glossary

Arctic	the region around the North Pole
asphalt	a black sticky substance (often mixed with crushed rock to make roads)
dome	a structure shaped like half a hollow ball
floor plan	a drawing that shows the layout of the areas in a home or building, as if seen from above
hearth	part of the floor where a fire is made or cooking is done
marshes	wetlands or swamps
mold	a hollow object that soft or melted material is poured into
spirals	curves around and around, into the center
thatch	grass, straw, or leaves, often used as a roof covering
traditional	used for a long time by a particular group of people or in a particular area

Index